LET'S FIND DIGIMON

SCHOLASTIC INC.
New York   Toronto   London   Auckland   Sydney
Mexico City   New Delhi   Hong Kong

Produced by Southern Lights Custom Publishing

12 11 10 9 8 7 6 5 4 3 2 1   0 1 2 3 4 5 6/0

Printed in the U.S.A.
First Scholastic printing, December 2000

LET'S FIND DIGIMON!

You can have fun with this book by yourself, or with your friends!

Here's how to find the Digimon hidden on these pages...

1) Look at each picture. The clues in the box will help you find the hidden Digimon.

2) If you can't find any of the Digimon, look at the answers on pages 31 and 32.

3) The Bonus Puzzles on page 30 have more hidden Digimon for you to find! You'll have to look through the whole book to find them.

4) If you need help finding the Digimon in the Bonus Puzzles, the answers are on page 32.

NOW, LET'S FIND DIGIMON!

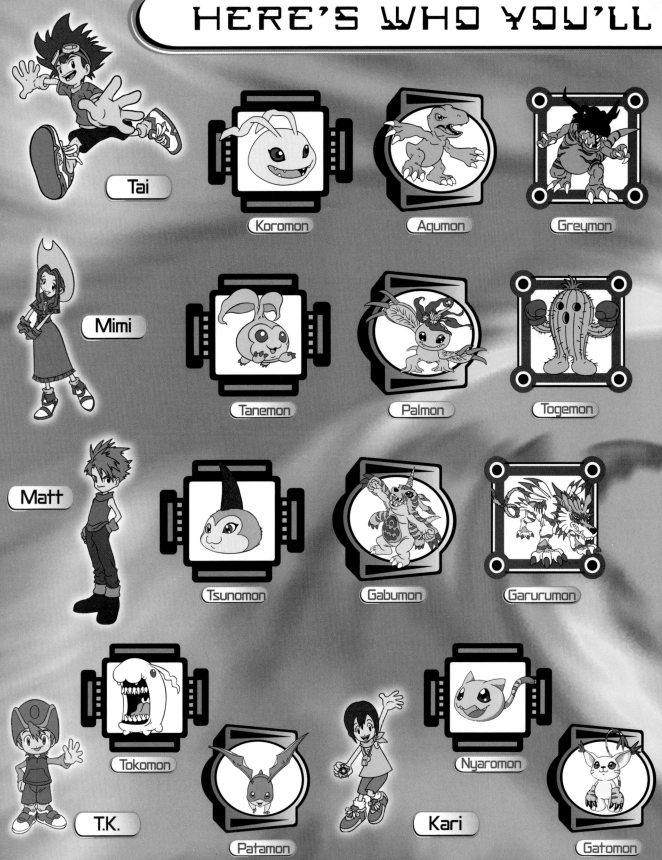

Tai

Koromon

Agumon

Greymon

Mimi

Tanemon

Palmon

Togemon

Matt

Tsunomon

Gabumon

Garurumon

T.K.

Tokomon

Patamon

Kari

Nyaromon

Gatomon

MEET IN THIS BOOK!

Sora

Birdramon

Biyomon

Yokomon

Kabuterimon

Tentomon

Motimon

Izzy

Ikkakumon

Gomamon

Bukamon

Joe

LOOK OUT FOR THESE DIGIMON CHARACTERS, TOO!

Elecmon

Wizardmon

Pixiemon

Gennai

Etemon

ANDROMON'S FACTORY

Andromon has been freed by the kids and their Digimon. But now, will he attack? Find Tentomon, Motimon, and Kabuterimon and help the kids escape!

Tentomon

Motimon

Kabuterimon

TOPSY-TURVY TOYTOWN

Look out for Monzaemon, the giant Teddy Bear who rules Toytown! Can you find Tai, Mimi, and Palmon before he does?

Tai

Mimi

Palmon

BAKEMON CHURCH

How many Bakemon ghosts can you find at this spooky church? Now find Joe, Gomamon, and Sora, and help them fight the Bakemon!

Joe   Gomamon   Sora

PRIMARY VILLAGE

You've arrived at Primary Village with T.K. and Patamon. Elecmon wants to fight! Find Gabumon, Tokomon, and Elecmon to help T.K and Patamon get away!

Gabumon   Tokomon   Elecmon

INFINITY MOUNTAIN

On the way to Infinity Mountain there are many Digimon. Some good — some evil! Can you find Patamon, Tsunomon, and Matt?

Patamon   Tsunomon   Matt

KOROMON VILLAGE

The Pagumon are holding the Koromon villagers prisoner! Can you get through and find Etemon, Tai's Crest of Courage, and Tai's own Digimon, Koromon?

Etemon

Tai's Crest of Courage

Koromon

CRUISE SHIP

A cruise ship in the middle of the desert? How did you and your Digimon friends end up here? Quick, find Gennai, Mimi's Crest of Sincerity, and Togemon!

Gennai

Mimi's Crest of Sincerity

Togemon

ETEMON'S PYRAMID

Etemon is after the kids and their Digimon. You can help by finding Izzy, Yokomon, and Piximon inside Etemon's Pyramid!

Izzy   Yokomon   Piximon

VEGIEMON'S DINER

Don't stay too long at Vegiemon's Diner—
you might get stuck there forever, like Joe!
Help him get away by finding Demidevimon,
his friend T. K., and Bukamon.

Demidevimon   T. K.   Bukamon

GEKOMON FORTRESS

The Gekomon treat Mimi like a princess. But look out, here comes Shogunmon! Find Tanemon, Agumon, and Mimi's crown so the kids can escape!

Tanemon   Agumon   Mimi's crown

MYOTISMON'S CASTLE

You've made it into Myotismon's castle! Can you help the kids get through the gate to the real world? To do it, you'll need to find Gatomon, Izzy's computer, and Agumon's key card.

Gatomon

Izzy's computer

Agumon's key card

THE REAL WORLD

It's the real world at last! But Demidevimon has sent Gesomon to attack. . . . Can you find Tai's little sister Kari, Wizardmon, and the Digivice before Myotismon and his henchmen do?

Kari　　Wizardmon　　Digivice

BONUS PUZZLES!

1. There are lots of sewer-dwelling Numemon in Digiworld. How many can you find in this book?

2. Vegiemon is sunbathing somewhere in this book. Where?

3. Datamon appears only twice in this book. Can you find him?

4. Where can you find Joe sitting on a roof?

5. Where are Biyomon and Tentomon hiding in a tree?

6. Sukamon and Chuumon are hiding together. Where? (Hint: You can find them together in three pictures.)

ANSWERS

Andromon's Factory

Topsy-Turvy Toytown

Bakemon Church

Primary Village

Infinity Mountain

Koromon Village

Cruise Ship

Etemon's Pyramid

Vegiemon's Diner

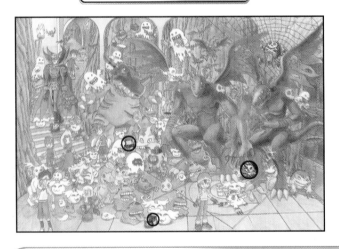

Gekomon Fortress

Myotismon's Castle

The Real World